ELSEWHEN

pieces

Robert Cowan

Illustrated by Ada Cowan

Paloma Press, 2019

Copyright © 2019 by Robert Cowan & Ada Cowan

ALL RIGHTS RESERVED.

No part of this book may be reproduced or transmitted in any form or by any means, electronic or mechanical, including photocopying, recording, or by any information storage and retrieval system, without the proper written permission of the copyright owner unless such copying is expressly permitted by federal copyright law. With the exception of nonprofit transmission in Braille, Paloma Press is not authorized to grant permission for further uses of copyrighted selections reprinted in this book without the permission of their owners. Permission must be obtained from the individual copyright owners as identified herein.

ISBN 978-1-7323025-6-3

Library of Congress Control Number: 2018955869

Cover image and interior illustrations by Ada Cowan

Book design by C. Sophia Ibardaloza

ALSO FROM PALOMA PRESS:
Blue by Wesley St. Jo & Remé Grefalda
Manhattan: An Archaeology by Eileen R. Tabios
Anne with an E & Me by Wesley St. Jo
Humors by Joel Chace
My Beauty is an Occupiable Space by Anne Gorrick & John Bloomberg-Rissman
peminology by Melinda Luisa de Jesús
Close Apart by Robert Cowan
One, Two, Three: Selected Hay(na)ku Poems by Eileen R. Tabios, trans. into
    Spanish by Rebeka Lembo (Bilingual Edition)
HAY(NA)KU 15 edited by Eileen R. Tabios
HUMANITY, anthology edited by Eileen R. Tabios
The Great American Novel by Eileen R. Tabios
The Good Mother of Marseille by Christopher X. Shade
Diaspora Volume L by Ivy Alvarez
Glimpses: A Poetic Memoir by Leny Mendoza Strobel

PALOMA PRESS
San Mateo & Morgan Hill, California, USA
Publishing Poetry+Prose since 2016
www.palomapress.net

for my ~~(ex)~~ ~~(step)~~ siblings

Rich, Janet, Ross, Will, Katie

CONTENTS

ACKNOWLEDGMENTS   7

VEILANCES   9

Morning Convictions   11
Attack Shirt Phone Refuge   12
Advice for Ninjas   13
Triple Negative   15
Strabo's Irritation with Hegel   17
Bird Meters   18
Return to Edges   19
Replacement for Words   20
A Visit to the Raccoons   21
Paratroopers in Space   22
Sky Black   23

LAMKIN   25

Lunch with Sisyphus   27
Vapors   28
Schlegel's *Me Against Greek Poetry*   29
Schedules   30
Unsettling Developments   31
Tides   32
Trekking with Shostakovich   33
Answers (to Follow-Up Questions)   34

FABULOUS DOSTOEVSKY CONFESSIONS   35

The Mouse and the Stove   37
The Dog and the Garbage Can   39
The Rabbit and the Ride-On Mower   41
The Hedgehog and the Fourth of July   43

SILLY MORALITY SONGS   45

Water Fountain Romance   47

German Secrets	48
Causualities	49
Pietà	50
Mallory's Lapse	51

ELSEWHEN 53

Sorry about that whole Rasputin thing	55
Folding Blonde on Blonde	57
Noise Machine	59
Bewilderness	61
Morts, petits et grands	62
Barnum's Gulag Fire Utopia	68
Khan & Kahn, Advisors to the Parasuicide Club	70

CONVEYANCE FRAGMENTS 75

Strands	77
Logics	78
Bardos	79

NOTHING TRAVELS INTO SOMETHING 81

ABOUT THE AUTHOR 93

ACKNOWLEDGMENTS

Grateful acknowledgment is made to the editors of the journals in which the following pieces appeared, sometimes in slightly different form:

Entropy (31 Aug 2017): "Folding Blonde on Blonde"

Flatbush Review 1 (Winter 2016): "Sorry about that whole Rasputin thing"

Green Spot Blue (13 Jan 2015): "Water Fountain Romance"

Here Comes Everyone 6.3 (Oct 2017): "The Mouse and the Stove"

Skidrow Penthouse 15 (2013): "A Visit to the Raccoons," "Replacement for Words," and "Return to Edges"

Word Riot (Nov 2012): "Attack Shirt Phone Refuge," "Paratroopers in Space," and "Vapors"

Thanks to Ashna Ali, Ross Alvord, Vanessa Baish, T.J. Beitelman, Eric Fortier, Denver Butson, Jennifer Hayashida, Jan Heller Levi, Richard Kaye, Yasha Klots, Cecilia Orphan, Nicole Ridgway, and Shanti Thakur for their valuable feedback on some or all of this manuscript. Thank you to Ada Cowan for her beautiful artwork. And thank you to Paloma Press' Aileen Ibardaloza-Cassinetto and C. Sophia Ibardaloza for their commitment to charitable work and for believing in these pieces.

Veillances

Morning Convictions

Awoken by a Caribbean man walking down the street,
rapping the windows open (mid-September),
not making out his words, just his inflection,

his vigorous accent, his fluid conviction.
New World black birds in the background
accompany him with sweet sounds,

with their red-tinged wings—
the wrong season for enticing mates,
maybe discussing politics—yet

seeming to lack the conviction of this man
who is fired up. But then, I listen. And I realize
the birds are aflame too, their tweets only sweet

sounding because their bodies are so slight
—just a few fragile ounces. Some actually
have thundering voices to their moved comrades,

for reggae singers misheard these three little birds,
channeling colonial fury with blood on their wings,
with their critique of the Old World.

And they are shouting at me now to listen
to this man, run out there and embrace him,
before he passes my window and flies away.

Attack Shirt Phone Refuge

We walk among brown stones. I in a white t-shirt,
she in a pink collar. She pulls to wait for a miniature
Doberman to cross the shadow-dappled street,

its owner a jolly Hispanic guy with short braids,
his girth obscured by a sail of black t-shirt
that reads, *Swallow,* in drippy lime letters

or it's goin' in your eye! As he checks
his messages, he ambivalently tells his yappy bitch
to stop jumping on my dog, who actually doesn't seem

to mind. Phone glow illuminates his double
stubble. She and I walk on. A smiley, well-scrubbed
couple in colorful t-shirts advances making earnest

eye contact. His is red with a robot silkscreen.
Hers is yellow and reads, *Je t'aime, Sunshine,*
with a cartoon girl in pigtails. They remark

how beautiful my old mutt is, as their puppy jumps
on her head, to her disgruntlement. They're so
friendly, I step back, and check my messages.

Advice for Ninjas

Watching the giant container ships come in,
driving to work on the Belt Parkway East
along the undulating water

between Brooklyn and Staten Island,
where the Upper Bay becomes the Lower,
before the Verrazano span,

I see a ship out there today
that doesn't say *Maersk* or *Hanjin*
or *CMA-CGM* on its battered hull,

a smaller vessel that reads *Japan Coast Guard*.
So brightly dislocated in their attempts
to navigate the ragged coast,

up over the ice bridge,
across the Bering Strait, and through
God knows what other divagations

to arrive here.
But then I realize
I can hear ninjas

giggling across the water—
over the obnoxious gulls,
over my own balding tires on the road

—ninjas who perhaps know more than I.
You see, there are slaves being
trafficked in those containers

and the coast guard ninjas
have followed them
from the origin of the sun

through the disappearing sea
ice here
to Goat Town,

doing good work,
these ninjas.
Yet I also know,

as I pass under the bridge incognito
in my own battered Volvo wagon,
that if they want to catch traffickers,

they will have to come up with
better camouflage for their boat,
erase the smug grins under their *fukumen*,

and stop snickering so loudly.

Triple Negative

When evasive Schrödinger introduced the concept
of negative entropy in 1944,
he was referring to how a living system

exports degeneration to minimize its own decline,
slowing the creep of decrepitude, not holding
onto lost youth so much as maintaining

a sort of equilibrium, the fight against boredom,
against sedentariness, contra lassitude.
Confused Brillouin, though, referred

to negentropy as something a system imports
and stores, which seems unlikely, since only
a few of us are lucky enough to revel

in disintegration, to celebrate the sweet decline
period of the cycle, to be brave enough
to embrace Śiva and not get soaked

by the Ganges River coming out of
his hair and into our sponge minds.
But whether you call it by these names

or others (syntropy, extropy, entaxy),
it's unkind. Why should someone else bear
the burden of your deterioration? It's like

sending your garbage into space—a forgetting.
But, were there a workable synthesis,
what would this amalgamated postulation be?

The opposite of entropy is the building up
of physical systems from something simple
with uniformly distributed energy

to something more complex
and non-uniformly structured.
Thus, the opposite of negative entropy

is positive order. A delightful, painful,
ambivalent redundancy. Because
after all, we reject chai with Vishnu

in favor of vodka with Gogol.

Strabo's Irritation with Hegel

In his *Geographica*, Strabo faults Hegel
for never having been to India at all,
like Heidegger's praise of Van Gogh

for painting a peasant's shoes
when he had really just painted his own shoes.
Strabo took issue with the formulation

that history began in the East
and will culminate in the West,
was irritated by the sheer superfluity

of Wilhelms and Friedrichs
in the Germanic states, had had enough
of those who claim familiarity with the exotic,

wondering why we can't be content
with facts of a more daily sort,
like that men like sandwiches

while women prefer soup.

Bird Meters

Chronometers tell you that hummingbirds hold
eternal mystery, at seventy beats per second,
regardless of your cloying skepticism.

Thermometers cause scorched ibises to step out
of ages when Saharan rulers strewed strangers with gold
that they would not reinvest in the stark future of Africa.

Tachometers point to when the mallard was aesthetically
edifying, when unhinged Kaisers only knew red
and black (too afraid of gyrating green and blue).

Barometers conceal the stress
of the woodcock after the kingpin has slipped
a splinter into its lychee head.

These ornithometers confirm our experiences
in waves or particles,
interstellar strings or ringing slaps.

But your history will only be grasped if you get
into the cockpit, take off the parking break,
and grab the throttle.

Return to Edges

Was it in that movie about Antonin Artaud,
or the one about Glenn Gould,
or the one about Wittgenstein?

A retreat to a stone house on the North Atlantic,
off of Newfoundland, among the Orkneys,
in Norway… or was it Greenland?

Maybe an inert structure edging the Pacific South,
around the frigid Magellan Strait,
hovering over Ross waters?

No.
No, it wasn't.
It wasn't there.

Somehow…
I know.
It was on Sakhalin.

Island of the reindeer people, the invaded Nivkh
of Yul Brynner, occupied by an army of convicts,
spoiled by oil and gas conglomerates,

island of gigantic ammonites I will try not to crush
during the Winter Bear Festival, which I will walk through
in silence, while shamans watch me suspiciously.

I will end there, in that rectangular house,
that two-room stone cottage, with that single steel bed,
that solid fir table, with salt-and-pepper beard,

and thick dark hair. In black suit and white shirt,
thin, with some hand-written pages,
an empty bottle, and a glass.

Replacement for Words

Boredom used to be disallowed;
it was for the unimaginative,
for the existentially challenged

for the febrile.
Now I am saturated
with eating, dressing, periodicals,

masturbation, design, weather, peoples
obsessions with ethnic anxieties,
American nostalgia for old versions of Europe,

with purple, and containers.
Let us not have a dog,
not know our history,

nor recognize any influences,
be compelled to disemploy words,
move toward the all-water: inhumanity

—past Germanics, beyond Inuits—
like that creature
with that word: *distance.*

We could replace even him
with spaces,
stillness,

movement.
We can fill
even the idea

of replacement
itself
with ice.

A Visit to the Raccoons

Iceland and Japan are volcanic islands
overstrewn with ghosts—translucent children
abandoned to solid raccoons. Tibet and Hopiland
are connected by a string through the center of the Earth

so that the desiccated ground vibrates in your sternum.
These four corners are one place, whose smudgy spectres
of young mammals are connected through their organ-chests.

When I visit there, I would like to feel that brittle howling,
listen to those little breasts. (It's not lost on me, however,
that children stop growing whenever the men in trump suits

at the saw-dusty table are out of bitter drink.)
Yet somehow, I find solace in the raccoons—
those shadow-images—creeping out, out from behind

the pre-pubescent skeletons,
for I'm not sure they're ghosts after all
... those children ...

just the distillation of my own bad habits,
their disappearance fixed by a man
at a smooth birch table

early in the morning.

Paratroopers in Space

I wasn't sure our ship was gonna make it...
low on oxygen, leaking fuel, plenty of rations, but no appetites.
It was hot as shit in there, as if we weren't sweatin' it enough.

And then, out the frickin' window...
What the fa... ?
It must have been some combination of exhaustion,

of sweating too much, not eating enough, lack of sleep.
It coulda been some kinda reflection off the glass—
not of something inside the ship

but maybe something... inside us.
But we all saw it. We all swear they were there.
Falling... in slow-mo... moving downward.

But alive. How the fuck were they alive?
In the vacuum of space. The freezing pressure.
The crushing nothing.

And what the fuck war were they fighting out there?

Sky Black

If there were no atmosphere,
if there were no blue sky,
no clouds, no vapor trails,

because the sky was black,
because we just looked out
into naked space, if we were

confronted, every single time
we looked up, with the reality
that we are alone

and infinitesimal in the expanse
of the galaxy, the universe,
the multiverse, the googolverse,

if our insignificance
confronted us every day,
so that we shrank, we shrugged,

we slouched away from actuality,
if we embraced the gravity
that holds us fast

to this precarious oblate
spheroid, this faulted faultless
freakosystem of blood and rock,

sinew and uncertainty,
would we dance, would we fade,
would we crouch,

and cry *There it is! The Sun!
The All-Shiny!* or would we
shrink, climb inside

artisanal bottles and smoking
mechanisms, to pause and stagnate
in denial, in denial

that our destiny is to appreciate
this green and blue stone?
If the sky were black,

then we would not embrace
black ourselves, not wear it
as a sign of passive revolt,

not create black in our factories,
not spew black in our rhetoric,
not stop short

at the color
that confronts us
everywhere.

Lamkin

Lunch with Sisyphus

Yma Sumac is playing in the background. How much time do you have? *Shrugs.* I mean before you have to get back to work? *Shrugs more acidly.* Thanks for meeting with me. I know you have a lot to do. When it took you guys so long to reply to the email, I thought this interview wasn't going to happen. I was so relieved when I finally heard back from your publicist.

So, I know your days have been well-documented: you push the rock up the mountain, you watch it roll down, you walk back down, and you push it up again. And I know that some have speculated about what you're thinking when the rock rolls back down. But I'm wondering more about the off-hours, about what you do at night, on the way to work, whether you have a family that you spend time with, whether Death ever comes by to taunt you. I see you've moved on to Carhartts from the loincloth Titian and all those other painters had you in. I didn't realize you weren't in Greece anymore. When did they let you work from Philly? Isn't it too flat here… for what you do? And why did you want to meet at a Brazilian place?

Vapors

Harold did love the shape of his skull. When he closed his eyes and ran his hands over it, from back to front, matting his hair forward, moving his hands so slowly and yet so loudly to his ears, forward, the shape was so pleasing, much sexier and more attractive, more handsome than how he might actually appear to the eye, his own or another, to the mirror. There was this parietal plane, between... ten and twelve o'clock, angled toward the moon, through the ceiling. It was so much flatter than the rest. Why? What did it mean? As his hands were forced against the grain of hair, his head was thrown back and he could feel. He could scarcely avoid the tendons, the vertebrae of his neck emerging from the open base like a coil—a biomechanical, Gigeresque whip. As his head reached the fullest extent of its arc and skins folded underneath his fingertips, he respected his skull's capacity to empty of thought, to drain along his spinal cord, into his genitals. The problem there, though, is that all those primal notions built up at the base, and the clogging caused coital vapors that traveled back up the pipe and begin to pollute the sink-cavity of the skull.

Schlegel's *Me Against Greek Poetry*

This Schlegel has been singing in a straitjacket for *Lucinde and the Fragments* since 1799. Prefers show tunes, mostly, but also does some Poulenc. Has written a lot of songs that are odes to movement as well as an enjambed, 1,046-line version of a Grand Master Flash song. Here, he imagines Mann's magic mountain as a gated retirement community in Florida, with eighteen golf courses, and explains that Aristotle's *Comedy* would solve all the problems of the Western world if we could find a copy of it. He's also been trying to find investors for some magazines for untapped markets: *Car & Wine*, *Yoga & Ammo*, *Negro Clogger*. Unfortunately, though, he has lost his edge since he stopped doing drugs. We'll see whether this new record heralds a come-back. Due out March 10th.

Schedules

Harold kept his nails short to prevent himself from picking his nose, which often bled. He wondered if people in more arid climates picked their noses more often than those in wetter climes. The related annoyance, though, was that toenails grow more slowly than fingernails, so he couldn't cut them on the same schedule. And these nail schedules did not match the hair, which had more than one schedule—one for cutting (monthly) and one for washing and conditioning (every day or so), the latter of which varied seasonally. (I won't even discuss the fucking shaving.) Beyond this was the moisturizing schedule, with its variations for face, cuticles, and body. Not to mention the occasional manicure—because his fingernails, like his father's, had a tendency to tear—or the annual pedicure in preparation for beach season. All of these overlapping calendars created a health and beauty cacophony that tended to cause Harold to just let his fingernails grow long so that he could silence the din by picking his nose while driving to work from Camden.

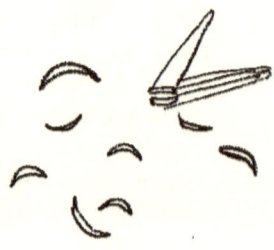

Unsettling Developments

Include Renaissance faires, Genesis (book chapter and band), Americans who mispronounce their own European surnames, letting the chain stores into Manhattan, that French internet terminology comes from the Québecois, baloney and its ilk, Merrells, the slackening of skin above my eyes, the rising price of Scotch, the ubiquity of Andean music in transportation hubs, memory's conflation of personal historical events, and decorative cabbages.

Tides

Harold enjoyed the feeling of defecating. The release from crowdedness. The destruction of barricades. The lifting of blankets. So that society could breathe again. And it was satisfying to see his contribution to this social meliorism resting in the embracing porcelain, as if it were glad to get out too, and fulfill its destiny. It was almost as if he could see the matter exhaling. Harold himself would be relieved that he'd gotten it done. Another thing off his seemingly endless lists—both "honey-do" and paper-related. But of course it wasn't done. Never. There would be plenty more crap to deal with. Every damned day. Relentlessly. Editors, sources, fact-checkers… If he were to survive, though, he would have to figure out some way to stem the tide. To stop the flow of all this shit. Somehow. Somehow it had to end. But of course the waste product wouldn't emerge if it hadn't fuel to convert in the first place. So perhaps he could not ingest any fuel, not eat at all—no processing, no waste. That would stem the tide. But then, eventually, his body would become eclipsed… and he would have to contend with another kind of diurnal movement.

Trekking with Shostakovich

Why he wore a black suit, I wasn't sure. It was rather hot, being September, and his black plastic glasses kept sliding down his hooked nose. We had to keep looking down, though, because navigating over the landslide was treacherous. (It's a long way to go for an interview, Lamkin.) He'd come to see the Tiger Leaping Gorge before it got so built up that it became unrecognizable. Yunnan Province had changed so much since he'd been here in 1976. All of China had. But Shostakovich wasn't ready for all the changes. Free-market-ish communism sounded promising, if seemingly contradictory. Musically, it could be very exciting, what with this "file-sharing." But where did that leave the state-sponsored artist? This was his primary concern. This, the upcoming weekend's performance of his 5th symphony on only Chinese instruments, and not completely destroying his Kirza artificial leather shoes.

Answers (to Follow-Up Questions)

Well, his ear was bleeding. She still had to get home on the subway. Our favorite had been the skinny-dipping on Christmas Eve. The cat remained dead. Alabaster was an elusive concept. Because Gore lost. Tom the mailman didn't even compare to Bob the mailman. We couldn't *not* watch *Touch of Evil* whenever it was on. You see, the piano was completely out of tune again. The tomatoes tasted sort of metallic. The colors looked shrill. So, geriatrics was where her heart lay. Jamal's callousness never ceased to amaze me. The Saab still ran pretty well. Though the PSI was always minus one. Because the sun is coming out again.

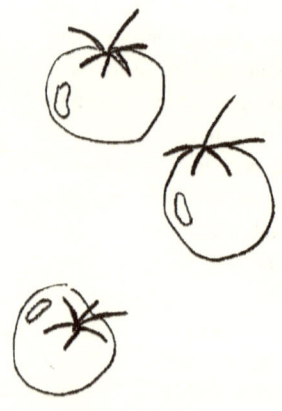

Fabulous Dostoevsky Confessions

Love the animals. God has given them the rudiments of thought and joy untroubled. Don't trouble it, don't harass them, don't deprive them of their happiness, don't work against God's intent.
— Fyodor Dostoyevsky, *The Brothers Karamazov*

The Mouse and the Stove

Dear fellow parent, my condolences for your terrible loss. I hope you and your family are doing alright. Please let me explain my position, though. There had been poop on the stove for weeks. For a while, I would just clean it up, but I knew eventually it could

make us sick to have feces where we prepared our food. I could think of no way to dissuade your family from using our stove as your toilet, so I finally decided, against my better judgment, to invest in "traps." I know; it's an insulting euphemism. I put out

traps with peanut butter, to no avail. With the cliché cheese, with no results. For weeks, the poop had all been the same size. Then, the other morning, two different sizes of poop—one regular, one small. I set out the traps with breadcrumbs. Early in the evening,

while we were still all up and about, I heard one go off. I went to look. A baby—yours, I presume. She was still alive in the trap. I'm so sorry, but as incredible as it sounds, I decided to leave her there to die. I didn't want to try to get her out to flush her down the toilet

or anything. Somehow that seemed like it would be worse for her. And me. But later, as we were winding down, there was crazed, high-pitched squeaking. I went to look. You were there trying frantically to free your dying child, as any loving parent would.

I don't know whether you saw me, but it seemed better to leave you alone together. Later, in the middle of the night—SNAP! I didn't go into the kitchen. In the morning, there were two intact traps still waiting with breadcrumbs—the one with your baby in it and an

empty sprung one. I went to pick up the one with your child in it. She moved slightly. Her eyes so wide, so vacant, shining like black pearls. I gasped, paused, and left the room for a few moments to collect myself. We were out of paper towels. I got toilet paper,

took the whole trap, wrapping it so I couldn't see her or feel her move in my hand, and deposited the trap with its dark cargo in the garbage. The sun came up and I felt crushed for you. You had come back for her, but there was nothing you could do but bear witness, stand vigil, as I would have done for my daughter. But now, it's evening again. We have enjoyed our dinner and I am cleaning up the dinner dishes. And I see the wild rice scattered among the burners of the stove. And it looks, to my eyes, like

gargantuan poop. Dostoevsky's Underground Man was bent on revenge for being insulted. But he felt that, whereas the normal stupid man can take revenge without obstacles, his opposite, the "man of acute consciousness," the "retort-made man," thinks of

himself as a mouse, even if no one else does. Thus, he would seem in sympathy with you. This acutely conscious mouse, though, doesn't believe in the justice of his desire to vent spite on his assailant and succeeds only in creating doubts and questions for

himself. Just as I initially questioned setting traps for you. The only remedy for this self-interrogation, though, is to dismiss it with a wave of one's paw and creep back into one's stinking mouse-hole to stew in everlasting spite. I, however, am not a mouse and

not a man of acute consciousness. I am just a stupid normal man of dull consciousness. And so I'm setting a trap for you tonight, as you would do for me. So you'll stop shitting where we make our food. And so you can be with your damned child. To look for

bread crumbs in some underground netherworld. Respectfully yours, Robert Cowan

The Dog and the Garbage Can

You lived "a dog's life," and I always wondered whether that was good or bad. For you, or anyone. We loved you and fed you and walked you. We yelled at you and kicked you and shamed you. Whom would you rather have been, Jaffa? Dog or non-dog? *In my*

mind, here in our Brooklyn apartment, with old hardwood floors with giant gaps between them, departed Jaffa stared back at me with an interrogative cock of her head, unsure what to answer, as a dead dog. My introduction to heroin was that night in

Northampton with Jim. I wanted to see what all the fuss was about, since it was so popular then. Although, I had remembered vividly that kid being rushed down the stairs and Mike shoving snow down his pants to shock him out of his potential O.D., so I was a little

nervous about it. *Jaffa didn't know what this had to do with dogs' lives, but she was too polite to ask.* So, we snorted some. And spent several hours walking around the abandoned insane asylum behind Smith College, eventually ending up unperturbed about

vomiting in the bathroom of the 1950s Blue Bonnet Diner. But in between all this, there had been the episode with the dog and the garbage can in Pulaski Park, by the Academy of Music. *Jaffa ticked her head to the other side, as if mocking the stereotype that*

dogs' head movements are funny. There was a stray dog curled up asleep. Next to a heavy steel mesh garbage can. Heroin had given me the feeling that I was invincible yet in harmony with the universe—a paradox that was transportatively delicious—but I

wanted to explore the more liminal spaces around morality, having recently read *Zarathustra* and deciding to glean that one can create one's own moral universe. So, I picked up the extremely heavy garbage can and held it up over the body of the sleeping

dog, which formed a cozy gray C. It seemed an eternity—of viciousness, of clemency—for the damned thing would have been crushed. It's ribs rising and falling so slightly on the edge of the cone of streetlight. My arms burned and Jim watched from up a tree, enthralled in anticipation of being disgusted, disgusted by the idea of being enthralled. Or so it seemed to me. *Jaffa stared at me, her eyes wide and penetrating, uncomprehending black pools. But her earnestness weakened me, as I remembered that we had had to*

put her down on Valentine's Day, when she couldn't hold herself up anymore, our dog of over 15 years. In that moment, I thought of a few years before, when I had lounged by an overgrown soccer field behind the medieval wall surrounding Siena, reading the

section in *The Brothers Karamazov* in which some boys feed a piece of bread that has a pin hidden in it to a dog, then watch the poor creature's agony gleefully. I remembered being so revolted by that. *Jaffa cowered, unsure whether she was ashamed of me for*

arriving at the garbage can idea or herself for being beholden to me. Or perhaps of Dostoevsky, for recounting that story. And the time just months before the garbage can incident, when I had used the same logic about creating my own moral universe and been

unnecessarily cruel to a girlfriend during a fight on the bleachers of a basketball court in Xi'an, under the guise of honesty. *J. blanked at me. Eager, inconclusive. Mostly just wanting to know that she was loved. And I paused. And I put down the mental*

garbage can. And said, I'm sorry. *And bent down for her to lick my face, ashamed for having burdened a dead dog with such pathetic humanity. And Jaffa just lay down on the floor, on her side, and stared at nothing in particular for a while.*

The Rabbit and the Ride-On Mower

Over a glass of wine, from across the floor, I explained to her, *As a child, I had a yellow rabbit's foot on a little chain. It was originally blue, but the dye came off in my Wrangler pocket and it had become a jaundiced yellow. It was a good luck charm, a*

testament to the idea that humans have better luck than, say, you guys. Rosalind hopped over, rearing back to smell my hand as I reached to pet her, then settling down, long veiny ears folded over her back, as I caressed each side of her. *I found out a few years*

ago—before you joined us—that rabbits like to build nests in tall grass in which to raise their young. She said nothing, avoiding making me feel stupid for not knowing this. *This was undisclosed to me, though, when we rented six acres in rural Vermont. And,*

one day, I was cutting the grass with the ride-on mower that came with the place... she stiffened, and my hand paused over her gray and white fur... *and I suddenly heard faint crazed squeaking, like crowds screaming at some distant historical event. I backed the*

contraption up and raised the blade. I dismounted, searched in the grass, and found six babies—all of them confused and upset. A mother lay beside them, still, a third of her skull cleanly shorn off, the remainder of her brain safely contained, like soup in a bread-

bowl. Rosie's eyes burrowed in, entrenched, one bearing down on me, awaiting my explanation. *A. was two and into bunnies and I wondered perplexedly how I would ever explain this horrible accident to her. There was only one humane choice. The car was in*

the shop and the only animal shelter was over 40 miles away. Across the driveway was a barren field, having recently been cleared of corn, where I had seen hawks swooping. I gathered the baby bunnies two at a time and, making three trips, deposited them

in the field, a little bit apart from one another so they wouldn't witness each other's demise. To be carried off. Into the sky. Rosie looked at me sidelong. Or maybe at the bookcase. Noncommittal about my avoiding responsibility for committing murder. *It was one of these horrible parenting moments. Of compromise. Of being unclear whether you're taking the civilized way through or the easy way out. Whether you're being a role model or a coward. It is that grappling with having constraints imposed on oneself.* Her

eyebrows arched, maybe. Then she settled again. *Like our caging our books off from you, so you won't dismember them. Like our not being able to leave the fruit bowl out, because you'll chomp the bananas.* She shrugged, imperceptibly. *But then again, I suppose*

we choose to impose those constraints on ourselves. She didn't respond. *Like Jack White setting up his stage inconveniently to keep himself on his toes. Like the Oulipo writers composing books with no E's in them.* She seemed intrigued, although I'd be at pains

to explain how. *Like their "N+7" constraint, of replacing every noun you would like to use by the seventh noun that appears after it in the dictionary, as is my benweed [OED 1971]. But L. calls me "Rabbit" and like you, and contrary to popular wisdom, I shit*

where I eat. You do this because you produce two kinds of feces: fecal pellets, which are waste, and cecotropes, which you eat secretly because they actually contain vital nutrients. I also produce two kinds of feces: shit, which is waste, and self-

destructive thinking, which makes life more exciting, and which I also have the good sense to engage in clandestinely. Rosalind extended her front paws, let out a pink four-toothed yawn, settled, and closed her eyes. I took another sip of my Bordeaux and

wondered to what Dostoevsky story this episode corresponded.

The Hedgehog and the 4th of July

There was a knock at my dacha door. Natasha, one of the young women I worked with, stood there rather primly with a small brown paper bag, bright blue eyes shining out from under her poorly dyed burgundy hair. The Belgian hedgehog to whom I was

recounting this chuckled quietly in his grass as we sat on the patio. *"It is your country's independence day!," she said. "What?" "The fourth of July!," she insisted, and shoved the bag at me.* Eh oui, le quatre juillet, he nodded, his whole spiny body curling. *I took the*

bag, which shifted in my hand, dubiously rustling a little on its own. With a big smile, with one gold tooth, she then turned on her heel and left. I stood there dumbfounded, unrolled and peered into the bag at the prickly back of a small living creature. I came inside

and left the bag open on the putrid-orange dacha floor so it could crawl out. "Huh! A hedgehog." Un hérisson? Oui. *I'd never actually seen one before, that I recalled, since there's no living species native to the Americas, our one genus having gone extinct*

in the Miocene. So named because they like hanging around hedges. Apparently, you guys haven't changed much in the last 15 million years, I added, looking around the bush-edged yard. *In Russian, the word for hedgehog— "еж"—is the same as the*

word for "urchin." Eh oui, en français, "un galopin." *Right, galopin. And so, what was I supposed to do with this galopin? Play with it? Let it hang around my dacha? You can't actually pet one, I figured, afraid to try lest the quills were barbed or*

something. So, I chose to try not to snuggle with it. It scratched around a bit, but I had no food for it (a) because I had no idea what hedgehogs eat and (b) because I really had no food in my room, which consisted of just a toilet, bed, table, and no chair. So,

after a little bit, I got into bed, read, the еж stopped moving, and I drifted off, remembering the night weeks earlier, around a campfire in the woods, how, amidst much draining of vodka glasses, many hedgehog jokes were told, the humor of which was lost on me. Je ne sais pas ce qu'ils veutent faire rigolo à propos des hérissons. Nous sommes plus serieuses que beaucoup de gens connaissent. Yes, I know you're more serious than most people realize. And I'm not sure what's funny about you either. But anyway,

around 6:00 AM, there was a familiar knock at my dacha door. I groggily opened and there was Natasha, fresh-faced and sparkly-eyed in the same navy-blue mock-Reebok track suit that she wore every day. She looked at me expectantly. "Ёжик," she demanded

pleasantly. "Oh, да," I said, collecting the еж and handing it over, a bit sorry that our strange night together was done. Et, alors, qu'est-ce qu'elle voulait avec tout ça? Well, I really don't know what the hell she meant by the whole thing. But, years later,

in a literature class with a chair of Slavic Languages, I asked, "So is there some tradition in Russian culture of giving a hedgehog as a present?" And, as it turns out, there is. He frowned approvingly, arching his dark eyebrows. *Besides Archilochus' aphorism about*

the hedgehog and the fox… The arch became questioning. *…that the fox knows many things, but the hedgehog knows one big thing…* An affirmative blink. *There is an example in Dostoevsky. In* The Idiot, *Prince Myshkin beats Aglaia at cards and she*

becomes furious, but the next day sends him a hedgehog as a peace-offering. Comme c'est bizarre. An urchin of peace, it seems. Buh. Je ne savais pas. No, I didn't know that either… much less knowing one big thing. The urchin pursed his lips in solidarity.

Silly Morality Songs
Frottola-Barzelletta Cycle

I. Water Fountain Romance
*For Warren, OH, where Halsey W. Taylor
invented the sanitary drinking fountain in 1912.*

Warren Ohio loves Halsey Taylor.
He envisions them frolicking,
like Mastroianni and Ekberg
in the freezing fontana,
he a mountain of man.

> *Love is a constant silent Noguchi fountain and
> he is the giant exploding Osaka Exposition water park,
> but his thirst lies unknown and unquenched.*

Their names imprinted, twisted
on a porcelain column, not
the statuesque tower of Malmö: Anita,
but the tower of London:
imprisoned Ohio.

> *Love is a constant silent Noguchi fountain and
> he is the giant exploding Osaka Exposition water park,
> but his thirst lies unknown and unquenched.*

Warren dreams wet dreams of crashing
falls, Victoria thundering across
shoulders, through his loin stream—
Zambia, the fetus of their
Zambezi, sheet-of-water child.

> *Love is a constant silent Noguchi fountain and
> he is the giant exploding Osaka Exposition water park,
> but his thirst lies unknown and unquenched.*

II. German Secrets

Marlene Dietrich knew that she could not sing.
She knew what black and white people appreciate—
that mute cigarettes corralled against her,
that men are, in fact, sleeping.

> *Such thoughts are whispered into our interstices,*
> *murmured to winds filled with black teas,*
> *but none shall know other than you.*

Arthur Schopenhauer's stylist had to take his head
to the Isle of Skye and plant it in the ground, so that
the winds of the North Atlantic could
sculpt his hair into a bird.

> *Such thoughts are whispered into our interstices,*
> *murmured to winds filled with black teas,*
> *but none shall know other than you.*

Joseph Beuys always wore that fishing vest
because coyotes don't have pockets, because
gristle slips, because otherwise, at night, the hat
would hang alone in the dark.

> *Such thoughts are whispered into our interstices,*
> *murmured to winds filled with black teas,*
> *but none shall know other than you.*

III. Causualities

A Diet of Worms decided the fate of
a sly translator in 1521, a key change
that took us one half-tone over.

> *One half is physics, the other certainly subjunctive,*
> *solid like Shandong furniture,*
> *elusive like sea glass on Mars.*

The Tokugawa Shōgun expelled
Europeans from Japan in 1639,
upset about a certain Jesus.

> *One half is physics, the other certainly subjunctive,*
> *solid like Shandong furniture,*
> *elusive like sea glass on Mars.*

Sakharov ironically died on the Day of
John of the Cross, in the year of the
crumbling walls, the century of dogs.

> *One half is physics, the other certainly subjunctive,*
> *solid like Shandong furniture,*
> *elusive like sea glass on Mars.*

IV. Pietà

Did you notice the ladybug that died in the Buddha's lap
this evening, after wandering his knees for days, hungry,
fighting the cold of Indian November?

> *Increasingly inert, no pain visible*
> *—British bird, American bug, all lady—*
> *resting on the leg of this prince.*

Some beetles have no spots, some with nine, some
spotless nine-spotted, some convergent. This one besotted
or frigid, over-wintering, on a kitchen window look-out.

> *Increasingly inert, no pain visible*
> *—British bird, American bug, all lady—*
> *resting on the leg of this prince.*

Many generations a year, however, infers that this lady
must be talked through the bardo of hearing, guided
past swarms of birds, and squashing children.

> *Increasingly inert, no pain visible*
> *—British bird, American bug, all lady—*
> *resting on the leg of this prince.*

V. Mallory's Lapse
After an etching by Robert Andrew Parker

Falling from 24,000 feet, body stomped into ice
piercing crystalline shapes of air. Leg broken.
Slipping slipping, where snowflakes don't plummet.

> *He knew not the tallest mountain is the top of the ocean streak.*
> *Whose flag is down there on that peak?*
> *Motherwell-elegy-black 'tis.*

Rising stars cancel glacial swim. Water freezes
around hopes and leaks expand to fit again. Descending
from pre-matter into matter, dark matter returns.

> *He knew not the tallest mountain is the top of the ocean streak.*
> *Whose flag is down there on that peak?*
> *Motherwell-elegy-black 'tis.*

Terrestrial fins soar. Frozen birds picking trilobites off
mountaintops, peeking into the mechanism through
which the subtle creature becomes gross mass.

> *He knew not the tallest mountain is the top of the ocean streak.*
> *Whose flag is down there on that peak?*
> *Motherwell-elegy-black 'tis.*

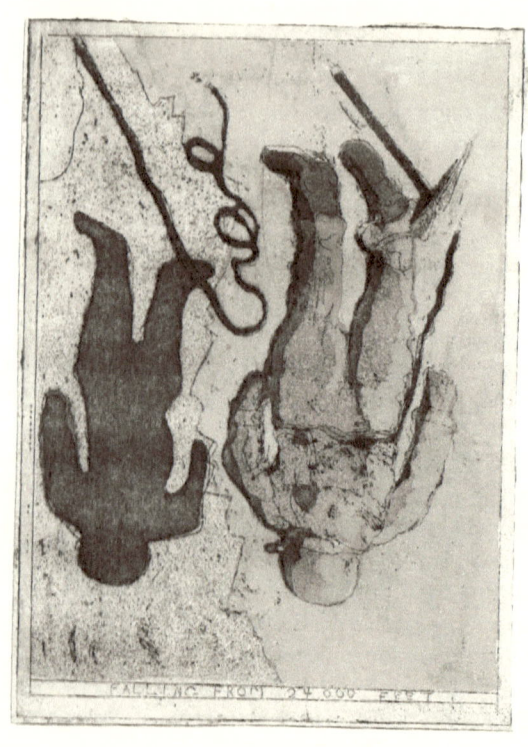

"Falling from 24,000 Feet" by Robert Andrew Parker (b. 1927), drypoint etching and watercolor on paper. Courtesy of Davis & Langdale Company, and Robert Andrew Parker.

Elsewhen

Sorry about that whole Rasputin thing

But I wasn't actually in the building.
Matt had lent me the Fiero to go see
Lisa in Northampton. Lezlie was just sitting
there with Grigori quietly braiding his hair

when he got the call to come to the palace.
Apparently, Grigori left in this blue embroidered silk
shirt and a beaver-fur coat and when he got there
they had this soundproof room in the basement

and *Yankee Doodle* playing on the gramophone.
Matt and Lynn were hanging out with that
Siberian shaman who lived in 3B. They had
gotten wicked baked and were listening to

Tuvan metal. They gave him *petit-fours* and
Madeira laced with cyanide. Lisa and I were
just watching a movie at her house around
then—*The Player*.

When Grigori wasn't dead after a couple hours
they just fucking shot him. He attacked them and fled
outside and they shot him again, in the forehead.
He fell into the snow and they started clubbing him.

Pretty much everyone who was still in the dorm
that night was on mushrooms, so who knows
how much help they would've been anyway.
It was like C# o'clock to Mike and Eugene that

whole night. They dropped him in an ice-hole in the river.
I'm sorry about the whole thing. Grig was a good guy.
A funny dude. I still can't believe how much beer
he could smuggle out of Price Chopper under his robe.

And like four cartons of cigarettes.
You must have some kind of *cojones* to do that.
But he had such a nonchalant air about it.
I didn't expect him to be treated quite so badly,

but really I didn't have anything to do with it.
I didn't realize that you liked him so much.
He did have a certain charisma…
even if he stole other people's lines.

Some called him *holy fool*
but I don't know if I buy that.
He seemed to me more like *clever devil*.
I picked up on some subtle cues about you guys,

but missed the bigger picture,
perhaps because you are *holy devil*
and I am *clever fool*.

Folding Blonde on Blonde

The infinite arrives barefoot on this earth.
— Jean Arp

*Clothing twists with repeated wear
and, when you fold it as clean laundry
you must choose: to fold it as it should be
or to fold it as it is*, thought Howard Danielsen

watching Carter's inauguration interspersed
with car commercials while folding clothes in
his bare feet, his hands turning with the liquid
precision of a crash dummy. *We spend our entire*

*lives driving toward death, resembling it, like
Arp's semblable, which means some blah-blah.*
The Mercury Monarch made him think alliteratively
of the Maserati, which itself sounded like a long stick

broken in several places, like he'd heard an old
Florentine man enunciate it once, criticizing some
skinny rich kid speeding off toward cypress shards.
Hence the association of the Maserati with the dead

James Dean, even though he arrived at his Cholame
California crash in a silver Porsche Spyder.
Bea had said, with her long blonde hair
draped seductively over her face, *You might*

get lucky later in the week, but How wasn't sure—
since they were phoenixes conversing on ignition
perches that may have had no sparkplugs—
whether the emphasis was on *lucky*, *later*, or *might*.

Disinterested in politics, she was in the other room
listening to Dylan's *Blonde on Blonde* and he
could see her through the French doors rubbing her
thumbnail against her lower lip while *Stuck Inside*

of Mobile with the Memphis Blues Again played
again. How preferred the smoothness of the
middle bone of his index finger against his upper
lip to something more like *Love Rollercoaster.*

But when Dylan asked, *Oh, Mama, could this
really be the end,* How knew that it could not,
for the irritating song would go on for sixty more
verses, and Jimmy Carter had only just been sworn

in, and Jimmy Dean had gotten stuck inside his
mobile with the Cholame Blues again. To avoid
such a fate, How wanted to go into the other room
and calmly, silently put the Dylan record back in

its sleeve and fold it like a shirt, snapping it crisply
each time, and run his fingers through his own
blonde hair, ensuring that he would not be folding
his blonde onto her blonde that night. He knew

the kind black-and-white peanut farmer would do
no such a thing, but would the technicolor movie star?
Dean was born in '31, Dylan in '41, and Danielson
in '51. Did '55 mark Dean's fall into paradise, '66

Dylan's stasis in purgatory, and '77 Danielson's
flight from inferno? Did significant things only
happen every eleven years? What would
happen in '88 or '99, 2010? Glancing up toward

Carter's hand on the Bible, invisible behind
the podium, How noted, *I am neither a great man,
nor do I come at the right time,* as an infinitely
black bra slipped his hand and arrived on his

bare foot. He picked it up slowly, felt the middle
of his index finger against its silk and lace
and folded its black on black, as it
should be folded.

Noise Machine

There is a noise machine by the bed
whirring away garbage trucks.
And there is a noise machine outside
my therapist's office, machines outside

all the therapists' offices, whirring
away confessions. It's Thursday night,
the night before bulk pick-up, and
as I walk from therapy, the smells. Oh!

The smells! For dogs—lovely. In late August,
that transitional smell between summer
and fall, when the urine smell of the city
is overtaken by some kind of late blooming

tree. It's now 9:47 PM, which I would like
to be my favorite time, because that actually
exists, but my favorite is really 9:74, which
is off-gray, and I don't know what to do

about that—nothing now, it seems
for I can't keep my eyes open anymore.
In my dream, I am driving to the Katonah
train station to pick up Tom Waits. I have

booked him to play at Book Court but I am
almost to the station and I realize that I haven't
arranged for any accommodations for him,
so I'm excited and trepidacious because he

will have to stay at my place and I hope
he's cool with that. I'll tell him I have a noise
machine. Before leaving for the train station
I had carried a clear bag of dog diarrhea

to the liquor store to buy whiskey and get
free dog treats. As I pass a construction site,
I am reminded by the plastic cabin that the world
is your toilet: Royal Flush, On-the-Spot,

Callahead. It was cooler out than I thought,
but the poop was warm and the feel of it
through the seemingly impermeable membrane
of the clear plastic bag was comforting.

Before sleep, having found in what is theoretically
mid-life that the jelly and the bread are superfluous
I had gotten into bed with a tablespoon
of peanut butter and some more whiskey

ready to drive to Katonah. Some people
pride themselves on knowing all the
different brands and flavors of scotch,
knowing which ones are too peaty or too tart

or too sour or whatever. I seem to have
weightier things on my mind, so that I don't
really remember whether that bottle was too
something, so that I am often surprised,

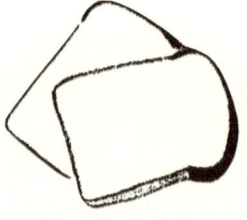

but not tonight, since it's cheap bourbon
anyway. But expensive peanut butter.
Mr. Waits should like them.

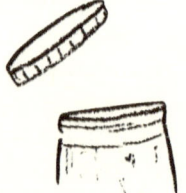

Bewilderness

The sane are insane in an insane world.
— Kurasawa, or maybe Diogenes

Pareidolia is a psychological phenomenon
involving an image or a sound stimulus
wherein the mind perceives a familiar pattern
where none actually exists.

The doors of perception stand before us,
their doorbell a standard black and white
rectangle of cheap plastic, although
I can't hear it over the whirring machine.

The problem is not with perception, though;
it is with processing all that data, and it's hard to hold
the doors open while you're running routines.
Hence the misfired questions:

- What makes the sea sweet instead of salty?
- Is the sky hermaphroditic if it's pink with blue clouds?
- Are bald eagles wearing baggy trousers?

And the word combinations that make us sad—

street trees, remind, narcopolis—which combine
into the sleeping city of another time,
when we mind the trees again,
separating them from streets

and stations, when we can stop
our whirrying, when we can be
alone together
and be wilderness.

Morts, petits et grands

They received a letter headed
Changes to Your Allsex Coverage,
the envelope so non-descript it almost
went into the recycling unopened.

Their policy would no longer cover
two sessions of half an hour per month,
with oral sex for her but not for him, and
no anal sex. Time, frequency, topography

and intensity had all been further reduced.
They saw on the chart that the highest rates
were for straight women, for they have
the fewest orgasms, the lowest rates for

lesbians, who apparently have the most.
He had been hoping to play skin tag with her but,
despite continuing to pay the same money,
this looked unlikely until at least next month.

You're, uh… not it, he thought.
They hadn't known that the solitude
in their marriage would be moderate to severe,
that they would forever hold their pieces

(perhaps because they had been to areas
where certain fungal infections are common).
Thus, quite a while ago now, they had both
increased their self-pleasuring, although,

even here, they would occasionally get stymied.
They were probably going through the motions
of going through the motions. They would flip
through their mental Rolodexes of standard

dramatis personae—past lovers of various kinds,
others they were attracted to, occasionally each
other—but they couldn't seem to get
sufficiently bandy-legged. So, then they went

not to the back catalogue, but beyond, to those
whom they never imagined schtupping before.
As they were both naturally stocky and
generally seemed to desire others who were

similarly endomorphic, they introduced
the opposite to their zones—those who were
much less pulcritudinous than they were
normally familiar with, boney even. And

invariably, new vistas opened up. People
they knew, whom they had never thought
about in that way, suddenly become the most
desirable objects imaginable. Suddenly,

that bearded guy she saw on the subway
reading in Korean made her come harder
than she had in years. And yet passing
such people afterward—in the hallway,

in the bodega, on the station platform—
would evoke little, for forays into the exotic
are usually fleeting, the damage they do
to either party willfully unacknowledged.

But this wasn't what was on her mind
after dinner, while he was doing the dishes
nor was the Allsex letter, actually. Instead
she was finally writing down a list she had

been composing since her shower that morning,
a list that popped into her head during meetings,
while answering e-mail, trying to use the damned
self-checkout at CVS. It was a list in reverse order,

like a Letterman count-down, that she wasn't sure
she would ever share with him:

> The Top 10 Places I Don't Think About
> 10. The Central African Republic
> 9. Andorra
> 8. Levels under the subway
> 7. Earth, TX
> 6. Deep inside our dog's ears
> 5. The nebulous ends of rainbows

      4. Globular Cluster 47 Tucanae
      3. The tops of my eyelids
      2. Cincinnati
      1. Your grave, my dear

Why this list needed to be made,

she couldn't say. And she still wasn't sure
she was done revising it. The order
was surprisingly hard to figure out.
Indeed, it had taken all day, as sequence

making often does, in between supposedly
more pressing concerns. It took mulling
over, marinating, time to gel. As she was

contemplating number one on the list,
he walked past her and lay down
on his side on the bed, unsure whether
to fall asleep reading or watching an action

movie with the sound turned off.
One of the books she was reading—
a young adult novel—lay open on the bed
and he stared at the edge of the page

sidelong, such a lovely warm yellowy
white in the dim lamplight. It said:

> behind
> filling her
> silence, then
> who *hide*
> close my eyes
> has made
> traitors—
> the lampposts
> all that is
> everything
> phone rings
> everybody*

---

*Beth Kephart, *Going Over* (New York: Chronicle, 2014), 110.

He didn't reflect on it, though, on whether
the "her" in the columnar snippet was *her*

or whom "my" indicated exactly. This was
not out of callous self-centeredness or
fatigue but because, with an unfortunate
weakness, he hadn't been able shake

the J. Geils song "Rage in the Cage"
he'd heard in the coffee shop that morning.
All day he'd remembered the giant college
marching band playing the '80s anthem

at midnight games in "The Cage"—
the basketball arena. As he'd filed into
the subway car that morning, he thought
about the phrase in German, imagining

his mother saying it quietly, over and over
while making sauerbraten: *Zorn im Käfig.
Zorn im Käfig. Rage is Zorn and cage is Käfig*
he thought, *so, John Zorn is John Rage*

*and John Cage is John Käfig. But without
der Zorn und der Käfig, they are just two Johns.*
In the men's room toilet, later in the day,
he'd noted, *Heidegger wrote Sein und Zeit.*

*Sloterdijk wrote Zorn und Zeit.
Rage and Time riffs on Being and Time.
Rage. Being. Times two. Is it time
to be enraged. Twice? By being, and time?*

*By philosophy and music? By the deaths
of our predecessors and the advent of
our successors?* He pulled his pants up,
giving himself a couple of extra shakes first.

Now, in bed, the day over, as his limbs
cracked into relaxation, he resolved to cage
in his own rage, to still his mind, and hear
music. But Handel, rather than Cage or Zorn.

Eventually she came to bed, after reading
more of a history of vulcanology she'd read

about in the Sunday book review months ago
and had finally been available at the public

library. She settled in, cozying; he opted
to pretend to be unawoken. She turned
on an action movie with the sound off,
to fall asleep to, envisioning erupting

volcanoes as the earthen-skinned
Marvel-comic Thing threw a car at someone.
She looked at the pages, remembering what
she had already read, and turned to him

as he began to drift off, twitching slightly.
She thought to him, *You are 'A'ā—
lighter brown and consisting of angular
chunks, the difference the result of your

flow dynamics.* He didn't stir. *You flow
rapidly, losing heat and increasing
in viscosity. Your history is powerful
and your background steep, so that

you move too fast to be smooth.*
No ankle crack. His sleep-state evinced
by the shallowness of his breathing.
Perhaps I am Pāhoehoe, she postulated.

*Possibly even darker… but smoother…
emerging with less force and over a
gentler slope, creating a ropy surface.
But ropes that cannot contain you…

for we differ in crystal and gas bubble
content. You advance steadily, as a single
unit that can bulldoze, while I propagate
individual toes, that surround objects.*

The cat walked by the corner of her eye,
but didn't look her way, much less join her.
"Pāhoehoe" sighed a long, stilted CO_2 escape,
the Allsex letter still sitting in the other room,

a diversion from deeper, more merciful
exhalations. *Were that we could both
be pillow lava, the result of our own
submarine eruption—bulbous, spherical,*

*tubular lobes—but we'd have to have
a lower effusion rate than we actually do.*
She knew this was true. *That would give
us enough time to form a thick crust*

on all sides of our lobe. He didn't nod.
*If we're not careful, though, we could
get caught up in a pillow flow and be
trapped in a pile up of lobes.* She smiled,

imagining the awkwardness, bordering
on disgust, of being piled up with other
couples they knew. She re-focused
her attention on the television.

The Fantastic Four was re-grouping.
He rolled back toward her, mouth agape
and snoring. She thought about what her
role would be if they were to form

a fantastic quartet with her brother
and her husband's best friend.
Fuck being the Invisible Girl, she thought,
even if she can make force fields.

Shit, I can make force fields already.
Her laugh faded. *I want to be the Human Torch.*
She looked over at him. *You are not
Mr. Fantastic,* although his snoring had subsided.

He can be the fucking invisible girl.

Barnum's Gulag Fire Utopia

The corner of Broadway and Ann Street,
Central Kazakhstan. Kengir inmates became
restless. Barnum's American Prison began
to burn, a spring day so frosty the tigers

could see their red breaths. After the murder
of some of the prisoners by guards, New York
saw one of the most spectacular fires in its history
—so much longer and more intense than Vorkuta

or Peale's conflagrations. Official record is hazy
on what year it was, but—a labor camp, a zoo,
a spectacle hidden—the revolution had begun.
Inmates proceeded to seize the entire museum

compound. Animals leapt from the burning
building only to be shot by Red Army officers,
the beluga whale charred in a pile of glass.
The museum of confinement burnt to the ground

and many of the animals walked the streets
of Manhattan, holding it for weeks, creating
a period of freedom for themselves unique
in the history of the Gulag. Kuznetsov,

Yegorov, and Dolgikh teamed up with
Paper Collar Joe, General Tom Thumb,
and the Fiji Mermaid—a rare alliance between
political prisoners, animals, true criminals,

and attractions. They forced the guards
and camp administration to flee and effectively
quarantined it from the outside. The prisoners
set up intricate defenses to prevent the incursion

of the authorities into their newly won territory.
This situation gave rise to the democratic
formation of a provisional prisoner government,
prisoner marriages, the creation of indigenous

religious ceremonies, a brief flowering of art
and culture, and the waging of a large, relatively
complex propaganda campaign against
the erstwhile authorities. After 40 days of freedom

on the island, intermittent negotiation, and mutual
preparation for violent conflict, though, the uprising
was brutally suppressed by the Soviet police
department with tanks and billy clubs on the morning

of June 25th. According to former prisoners and
Solzhenitsyn, 500-700 people were killed or
wounded in the suppression, although official
figures claim only a few dozen. Barnum soon

opened the New American Prison, which also burnt
to the ground in 1868 on a day so cold the water
froze in the firemen's hoses. That time the inmates
leapt into the sky singing Buryat folksongs.

Khan & Kahn, Advisors to the Parasuicide Club

Only the insane person takes himself very seriously.
— Max Beerbohm

If Flaubert's pedantic Bouvard and Pécuchet
had had twins with Hergé's bumbling Thomson
and Thompson, they might have produced my
absurd colleagues Khan and Kahn—one a Kafka

scholar turned college administrator who updates
his curriculum vitae as a form of validation;
the other, in his own view, *a teacher who writes*
rather than *a writer who teaches*—who's to say

which is more "impactful." One suffers from
compassion fatigue, the other from best practices,
a pair of zombies who work on the suicide floor,
the one that, every few years, a student jumps off of.

They are the faculty advisors to the Parasuicide Club,
bringing together those who contemplate (since
they gravitate toward each other anyway), sponsored
by the widow of their colleague who had his students

write suicide notes as a creative writing exercise,
and, the day they were due, was killed in a car
accident, a cloud of suicide notes around his smoking
car as the police pulled up. Their field is comparative

literature, but Khan and Kahn have to stop
comparing themselves to each other, have to stop
reading contributor's bios, for comparison is deadly.
For decades, Khan thought that he was amassing

what to say, when, in fact, he should have been
practicing how to say it. An autobiographical pact
with himself: to tell the story later. So, he just
stepped all the way into the car and watched

the closing doors. Kahn, by contrast, was still
in a civilian black t-shirt and jeans, a *hypocrite
écrivain*, trying to tell the stories behind scars
without telling the truth. *How do we know*

that wood doesn't suffer in the fire, he would
ask himself, when what he really meant was,
when will I feel like a success? As each
circumvented his own hang-ups, they had

nonsensical conversations, like teenagers
on drugs. Khan: "In the nineteenth century,
discoveries of mammoth remains were so
common that mammoth ivory became a major

export of Siberia." Kahn: "There are books
on stoops in the rain, like toddlers making
confessions of original sin." "I can't handle
music on shuffle while I am on the elliptical,"

said Kahn. "Soap is dirty," Khan agreed.
"Always be blue to yourself," Kahn concluded.
"Do immolated monks think about chocolate,"
posed Khan, noticing that it was already dark out.

At home, subject ruled object, accusative
and dative locked in struggle, as Kahn sat
at his laptop revising an article he and Khan
were writing together, always messing up me

and I, never sure which one he am, cursing
the necessity to mean, trying to create logic,
but making short work of coming up short.
Montaigne called them *essais*, from the verb

to try—attempts to absent himself from city life,
to re-embrace nature, attempts to be solitary.
But Kahn thought that writing does not arise
from the need to re-acquaint oneself with

the natural world, to put down the implements
of humanity and remember earlier selves,
to return to pre-progressive days, days
when each human wasn't its own universe,

when cycles were more easily discernible,
when gods' intentions were clearer, not
buying the idea that, if civilization is a failed
evolutionary experiment, the onus is on us

to be less human. Over clandestine whiskey
in their office, Kahn noted, "About two
thirds of the way through the semester,
a student of color says, 'I thought you

were just an uptight white guy.'" "Because
it's the first time they can see that
you have tattoos," adds Khan. "Or it's
the day that we have a frank discussion

about drugs," concedes Kahn. "Granted,
you are white and uptight," Khan avers.
"Our colleagues have always made fun
of my neat side of the office," Kahn concedes.

"A straight, upper-middle-class, Western-
European man is a dinosaur," stated Khan.
"Afraid of intersectionality, you cissy,"
challenged Kahn. They finally decided

it was time for the effacement of their
Indo-German collectivity, and went out
onto the balcony. "That McCandless kid
found that solitude must be shared."

"And Marx proposed giving up property."
"But wouldn't you like to be a literary
property?" "I don't know. I didn't finish
Don Quixote or *Tristram Shandy*."

"I didn't finish *The Magic Mountain* or
In Search of Lost Time." "Perhaps we
should go in search of our own quixotic
magic shandy." "Good idea." And with that,

they went to the balcony edge and clasped
hands, like diapositive artists ready to leap into
the void. They took a deep breath together
and exhaled. Then they turned and smiled

at each other, their weekly ritual-meeting
complete. "Ok. Ready for that drink?"
"Yup." But that night, Khan sat up
a long time finishing their co-written article,

trying to get right the closing for its
submission: *Thank you for considering
our work, We look forward to hearing
from you, Theoretically yours,*

Best, Bets,
Beset, Beast,
Jest, Just,
K. & K.

Conveyance Fragments

Strands

An overnight layover. As I try to sleep on a set
of connected pleather seats, the only bank
of televisions that are on—25 of them, five-by-five—
loops a half-hour program twenty-eight times,
about the humble but glamourous Princess Diana,
because Virgin Welcomes You to Gatwick.

My orange-haired, blue-eyed companion
is stared at by all those present, for the 48 hours
from Beijing to Xi'an, but the goats are not annoyed
that the rail counter lady wouldn't sell us higher-class tickets,
because they know that communism provides
little incentive for empathy.

Two big smelly German feet in the face
on a crowded sleeper-train from Brussels to Budapest
in the Fall of '89 symbolize two halves reunited
to give Western Europe, and me, a familiar bitter scent,
in case you had forgotten that politics is malodorous.

After sweaty screaming matches with sari vendors,
the cranky American consulate, and the pudgy
and mustachioed Central Intelligence Division, who
inform me that I am *not a gentleman!*, we get out of Delhi
for Christmas with passports, minus exit visas,
wrapped around an inch-thick wad of rupees.

A trucker drops me into a flying 4:00-AM Citroën
blasting Earth Wind & Fire to leave me at the Paris
périphérique, but I wake up inside the ring. Hitching
out of town at rush hour proves impossible, so I crawl
under giant hedges outside Versailles to sack out,
unbeknownst to Marie Antoinette.

A six-month-old baby, a flight delayed for seven hours
at the gate—no bathroom, no food, nothing to do, nowhere
to go—Rio de Janiero. The husband becomes mostly useless
in this context, which demands much breastfeeding,
much, smoothing, much pacing, little Carnival.

Logics

Two competing generals, who apparently own the planes,
run the two flights per day from Chengdu to Lhasa.
They are five minutes apart: 8:00 AM and 8:05 AM.
We miss both. And go to get Szechuan food.
For breakfast. Befuddled, but looking forward
to ginger, garlic, chilis, if not yet Tibet.

A Scottish football club gets us drunk with haughty
raw assertions that embarrass proper fellow passengers
on the ferry from Oostende. In our dank London hotel,
the news update shows them destroying a train car
at the Dover depot, because, we agree, that needed to be done.

On Royal Nepal Airlines from Kathmandu
there are no assigned seats, so Indian passengers swarm
around the glass doors 40 minutes in advance and finally
rush the plane, where the smiley dark man greeting us
at the bottom of the stairs wears a baseball hat
that reads TITANIC.

The Fundy tide goes down over 53 feet and boats hang
in suspended dry-dock animation over endless alien mudflats,
but we know, despite our borrowed Lexus SUV, that we
cannot outrun it, for Lexi don't float any better than I do,
despite being a sort of New Scot.

Extra fees paid for overweight baggage piled in the aisle
on Aeroflot to Yekaterinburg. A thunderstorm strobes
my and a trembling man's faces as we consume all
the chocolate and vodka the stewardess has. When the lights
finally come on, a screw falls out of the ceiling onto my face.

Tiny Golden Rock Airport in Basseterre. Nevis?
St. Kitts. My teenage friend's parents look at each other.
Where do we pick up the car? Apparently, it's the blue one.
There's only one car in the parking lot. And it's blue.
And the key's in the ignition. And it's almost out of gas.

Bardos

Hitching in a semi down out of the swirly drop-off Alps.
Once flat—*nulle part*, the middle of the night—
the trucker pulls far off the highway, stops supposedly
to gas up, says nothing and vanishes for a full hour,
murdered by darkness, or so I nervously assume.

Trivandrum to Mumbai. They said it was a 24-hour ride—
not 44 hours, with no walkman and no book—to think
about the passport, cash, cheques, and cards lost to that lightning
ghost boy in flip-flops who materialized out the corner
of her eye from an empty platform.

The thirty Italian books in my giant backpack make it
unscathed, thumbing it from Siena to Le Havre, until the heavens
open during the last 100 meters to the dock. I would not
even attempt to peat-dry Ginzburg's *Vita Immaginaria*
in the cozy apartment in Donnybrook, Dublin.

Seven days on rails of flu-flattened pallor, sweating
out small salted cucumbers and bland Siberian sausage,
staring at xeroxed conifers and choking industry,
from the Baltic Sea to the Gobi Desert, longitude
more comprehensible with each successive day.

In the Formosa Strait, we stand on the rusty white deck
with British doctor-to-be Lancelot Turtle and men inside smoke
toxic nubs, grumble over elephant chess, and slurpe noodle soups,
while flying fish surge up into the rushing saltless vacuum.

On the narrow craft corking on irritated waters
between Inishmore and Inishmaan, the captain stands still
among the Galway Bay tumult, his belly impervious to spray,
his cap seeming to have never been removed, his Aran sweater
apparently the source of all his power.

Nothing Travels Into Something

The void began in Magadha, almost two and a half millennia ago. It began to feel

                                      empty. A creeping feeling. As if

sacred figs had backed themselves up in its gut and then rotted until they vanished completely,

        leaving a slimy, leathery residue.

                            The streets of Pataliputra –
named for the bodhi, for a raja's daughter, inside the giant fortification walls and wooden tresses that Ajatashatru had made – seemed

eerily silent over the actual din of city activity. I don't think it was because Ajatashatru
was a conqueror (ironically a contemporary of Siddharta), but
        because, under certain conditions,

                                        substance fails to form
into anything digestible.

        When the void moved on
                to third-century Alexandria, it found that

the magistrates were not cool with the vacuum. Origen and it

                hopped into a jeep

but the officers at the checkpoint reminded them

      that the sacred was not allegorical,
      god was not logos,
      and animals were not reincarnated until they became humans
                and then joined the divine.

Most of the prevailing views left no room for it,
                for its emptiness,

      but Origen's did,
           for knowledge implies lack and lack implies filling.

        So, they went to a fig restaurant and had figs.

    Taking a thousand years to get to Bagdad was unwise, though;

it should have gotten there sooner.

    But it takes a surprisingly long time for void to travel through timespace, particularly with so many detours.

And you have to understand twelfth-century Bagdad, before the Ilkhanate Mongols
  took down the Abbasid Caliphate—

      Indian mathematicians had made zero the embodiment of the void.

  Ibn Rushd had defended Aristotle against encroachments from atomistic thinking,

    so Muslims had to choose between Aristotle and the void,

       and, happily, they chose it.

In Renaissance Tuscany, though, it vanished again,
      which was precisely the point. Ha-ha.

          Compressed to a final originary moment.

                It was all Brunelleschi's fault. It stepped
inside the Florentine Baptistry,
                    and was just gone.

          Alberti did get it out, but it took a couple

     decades, emphasizing planes rather than cones and rods.
Bad vision.

      But the void didn't really want to be gotten out.
          It preferred its face pressed up against the marble

                not sure who was using it.

At Jena, the idealistic Jacobi railed against it,
employed his critiques of it against others, supposed
"nihilists," whom a Lutheran pastor had identified.

                        Fichte picked up on this, after the two
went drinking in Baden-Baden, I heard, but he eventually
                retreated into its fold.

It all seemed so political, so much less to do
                 with faith in transcendence. Made me

      want to rinse the sand off my contact lenses.

        Some saw the new Russian men that followed

about seventy years later as a cautionary tale,

    of what the void as social policy could become,

        from land and liberty to houses and fire.

            The serfs were freed, the aristocrats
    became superfluous,   forces burst forth—

as I saw on Petersburg's trolley cars

                —and were sent to Siberia.

        Later,

                outside the prisons of Paris, cocky

slant-faces appropriated those who were braver than they, brave enough

        to embrace the void. Petty thief, petty Catholic, pretty boy, pretty.

Who did that philosopher think he was?

        Co-opted the prisoner, just as he'd co-opted blacks and Mao Tse-Tung.

            As if Mao needed him. As if white faces didn't slant on their own,

                bilateral symmetry being bullshit.

                In 1940s New York, that junkie
                showed the void his tommy gun,

which was all fine until those bongo-poets showed up. The subway beats us all into submission,

just as I hoped to do with some of them.

                              The ones out in the woods, the ones who kept at it for real,

        they were ok.

                              But the ones who didn't understand why
    more girls
                                    didn't want to lay them, they were
    for smacking.

Or at least for impressing silence upon,

                                          as it attempted to do.

When it arrived in London in 1970,

                         it realized just how little attention

      it had been paying to physics. So wrapped

up in religion and philosophy, acting so old-fashioned, with such hold

                 over views, held over itself. But those
smug young Brits

brought about a singularity

               —non-rotating, uncharged black holes.

                       They were
beautiful.

     The void felt neglectful, derelict of duty.

     Why hadn't it faciliated these?
     Why hadn't it done better?
     Why hadn't it done…
                less?

                     Why not nothing?

Lately, though,

                Kinshasa has shown us a new way,

    forcing us into a world-historical, a cartographical question mark. Now

        it has become apparent that the opposite of the void—its twin,
            but not its doppelgänger—

                      is the infinite.

          Thank fucking God.

I don't know why it's comforting, but somehow, cozily,
    I feel like I can finally stop worrying about the void, monitoring
        its perambulations.

        I can finally stop and relax.

                      Into something.

About the Author

ROBERT COWAN is a professor and dean at the City University of New York, and a volunteer instructor at Rikers Island Correctional Facility. He is the author of two hybrid-genre collections—*Elsewhen* (Paloma Press, 2019) and *Close Apart* (Paloma Press, 2018), and two monographs—*Teaching Double Negatives* (Peter Lang, 2018) and *The Indo-German Identification* (Camden House, 2010). His poetry, fiction, creative nonfiction, and scholarship have appeared in various journals and anthologies.

About the Illustrator

ADA COWAN is a Brooklyn-based artist and photographer whose work has appeared in National Public Radio's *The Salt*, *Sierra*, *The Washington Post*, and books by Paloma Press and Peter Lang. Currently a student at the NYC iSchool, Ada has studied at the Fashion Institute of Technology, the Frick Collection, the Museum of Modern Art, Pratt Institute, and the Whitney Museum of American Art. Her work has been selected for Arts Connection exhibits three times and profiled in *Time Out New York Kids*.

Established in 2016, **PALOMA PRESS** is a San Francisco Bay Area-based independent literary press publishing poetry, prose, and limited edition books. PALOMA believes in the power of the literary arts, how it can create empathy, bridge divides, change the world. To this end, PALOMA has released fundraising chapbooks such as *Marawi*, in support of relief efforts in the Southern Philippines; and *After Irma After Harvey*, in support of hurricane-displaced animals in Texas, Florida and Puerto Rico. As part of the San Francisco Litquake Festival, Paloma proudly curated the wildly successful literary reading, "Three Sheets to the Wind," and raised money for the Napa Valley Community Disaster Relief Fund. In 2018, the fundraising anthology, *Humanity*, was released in support of UNICEF's Emergency Relief campaigns on the borders of the United States and in Syria.

www.ingramcontent.com/pod-product-compliance
Lightning Source LLC
Chambersburg PA
CBHW021638080526
44584CB00015BA/1520